SNAKES

ERIK D. STOOPS &
ANNETTE T. WRIGHT

Sterling Publishing Co., Inc. New York

Library of Congress Cataloging-in-Publication Data

Stoops, Erik D.
  Snakes / Erik D. Stoops and Annette T. Wright.
        p.   cm.
  Includes index.
  Summary: Questions and answers explore the world of snakes, their
physical characteristics, behavior, and interaction with people.
  ISBN 0-8069-8482-1
  1. Snakes—Miscellanea—Juvenile literature.   I. Snakes—
Miscellanea.   2. Questions and answers.   I. Wright, Annette.
1961–   . II. Title.
  QL666.06S8757   1992
  597.96—dc20
                                                        92-16995
                                                        CIP
                                                        AC

Cover photo: West African
Bush Viper by James F. Brown,
Courtesy of Fort Worth Zoo

Design by Judy Morgan

2   4   6   8   10   9   7   5   3

First paperback edition published in 1994 by Sterling Publishing Company, Inc.
387 Park Avenue South, New York, N.Y. 10016
© 1992 by Erik D. Stoops & Annette T. Wright
Distributed in Canada by Sterling Publishing
% Canadian Manda Group, P.O. Box 920, Station U
Toronto, Ontario, Canada M8Z 5P9
Distributed in Great Britain and Europe by Cassell PLC
Villiers House, 41/47 Strand, London WC2N 5JE, England
Distributed in Australia by Capricorn Link (Australia) Pty Ltd.
P.O. Box 6651, Baulkham Hills, Business Centre, NSW 2153, Australia
Printed and bound in China
All rights reserved

Sterling ISBN 0-8069-8482-1 Trade   ISBN 0-8069-8483-X Paper

CONTENTS

HOW SNAKES LIVE
4

THE SNAKE'S BODY
14

THE SNAKE'S SENSES
28

EATING HABITS
34

SNAKE REPRODUCTION
44

SELF-DEFENSE
58

SNAKES AND PEOPLE
66

GREAT SNAKES
72

INDEX
80

HOW SNAKES LIVE

The snake is a very weird creature. It has eyes that don't blink, odd-looking skin, and strangest of all, no legs! How does it move? How does it eat? These questions get asked all the time. Here are some answers.

By Shay Hamper

◄ This yellow snake is actually a baby Green Tree Python. It will spend nearly all its life in the trees.

By David T. Roberts, Courtesy of Dallas Zoo

◄ Because they are so heavy, most snakes with big bodies, like this Dumeril's Boa, have to live on the ground.

By Donald Hamper

◄ Carpet Pythons got their name because they resemble oriental rugs. They blend into their surroundings very well.

► Whipsnakes are very common and active. They are always on the move.

By Jeffrey M. Howland

What is a snake?

A snake is a creature that is made up of a head, a long body, and a tail. It is considered a reptile because it has scales and is cold-blooded.

►This Wagler's Palm Viper is just one of the thousands of unusual snakes found all over the world.

▼ Reptiles do not have fur or feathers on their bodies. This Eyelash Viper clearly shows the scales that all snakes have.

Is its blood really cold?

Not really. The snake's inside temperature is the same as the temperature of the air and ground. Snakes can die if it is very hot or cold, so they find hiding places to protect them from the weather.

For example, a snake will bury itself in the dirt or hide under branches, bushes or rocks to stay cool. In the morning when it's cooler, snakes come out of their hiding places and sit in the sun to get warm. In the afternoon they find shelter from the heat. They may come out again at night, after it cools down.

What does a snake do at the North Pole?

Nothing—there are no snakes around the North or South Poles, where it snows most of the year.

By Jeffrey M. Howland

▲ When snakes lie out in the sun, it is called "basking."

▼ Many snakes, like this Narrow-Headed Garter Snake, rest in water so they can stay cool in the summer heat.

By Jeffrey M. Howland

7

Does a snake shiver or perspire?

No, a snake doesn't do either one. Mammals shiver to increase their body temperature when they are cold, and perspire to cool off when they are hot. But the snake's temperature is the same as the land around it, so it must get out of the heat or cold to prevent damage to its body! Life can be dangerous for a snake living in the desert or on a mountain!

By Donald Hamper

▲ Some snakes can live in cool temperatures and even swim in cold water, like this water snake.

What about pure white snakes? Where do they live?

A snake that is pure white or with a lot of white in its coloring is sometimes called an "albino." This kind of snake will probably not live very long in the wild, since it can't blend into the colors of the land the way most snakes do. Albinos are often caught by hunters for food, or taken in as pets or put in a zoo.

▲ Albino means "without normal coloration." This Albino Diamondback Rattlesnake would have difficulty blending into its surroundings because of its light color.

▲ White snakes, such as this Python, are very rare. This snake is not a true albino, because it has dark eyes.

▶ Albino snakes are not always completely white, but may be yellow or orange with pink or pale yellow eyes.

9

Are snakes found everywhere?

Almost. The only places that snakes don't live are on the tops of very high mountains, at the poles, and in Ireland, Greenland and New Zealand.

Of course, you won't find snakes in big skyscrapers in the city, unless, of course, people bring them into their offices!

▲ You can usually find plenty of snakes where there are rocks, bushes and trees. "The Boulders" National Park in Australia is home to many snakes.

▶ Snakes are also found near rivers, as in this area in Rio Sonadora, Puerto Rico.

By Jeffrey M. Howland

By Jeffrey M. Howland

10

Where is the best place to find a snake?

Imagine yourself as a small, skinny little snake that is afraid of getting lost in this big world. You need a place to hide and sleep, to find food, and to have a patch of sunlight once in a while to get warm. Where would you go?

- Under a rock or log
- In a tree or bush
- Underground or in a cave
- Near a lake or in the ocean
- In the desert or the jungle
- Under a house or in a flowerbed

In fact, just about anywhere at all!

By James F. Brown, Courtesy of Fort Worth Zoo

▲ Snakes such as this Louisiana Pine Snake may hide under rocks or beside them. They will frequently warm themselves on a rock in the sun.

By Jeffrey M. Howland

▲ Many snakes, such as this Rough Green Snake, live in trees and bushes or in leaves on the forest floor.

By Jeffrey M. Howland

▶ Many snakes, like this Cottonmouth, live in the water or around it. This snake is also called a Water Moccasin.

What do snakes die of?

Snakes can die of old age or because they are attacked by another animal. They can die if they can't find enough to eat or drink. They can get sick from diseases or from being too cold or too hot.

They can also be injured by falling out of trees or crushed by falling rocks, and especially by being run over by cars.

Why do snakes get run over so often?

Snakes like to rest on black-top roads, especially at night, because the road is warmer than the rest of the ground. Snakes do this by instinct, and they are not fast enough to avoid the cars. Unfortunately, we can't explain this to them, and many do indeed get run over.

▲ Many snakes, like this Racer, are small and delicate and easily become prey to birds and mammals.

▶ You can often see snakes like this Hooded Snake crawling along the sandy ground beside roads. They go there to get warm.

How long do snakes live?

If a snake were never to have an accident or get sick, and if it could always find enough food to eat, it would be able to live anywhere from 30 to 40 years, depending on the species.

If I want to see a snake, where should I look?

The best places to see snakes are in pet stores, zoos, or museums.

It is not safe to look for snakes under rocks and shrubs and other places where snakes hide. If you disturb them, they become frightened and may bite to protect themselves. Snakes have an important job to do—eating rats, mice and other animals—and need to be left where they are, in the wild. That way, nature will be in balance, just as it's supposed to be.

If I want to be a scientist and study snakes, what will I be?

A scientist who studies animals is a *zoologist*. One who studies snakes and other reptiles is called a *herpetologist*. One who works with sick animals is called a *veterinarian*.

By Roberta A. Kayne, Courtesy of Fort Worth Zoo

By Donald Hamper

▲ You can see snakes like this Uracoan Rattlesnake in zoos and in some museums, where they are safe to look at up close.

▲ An Albino Pine Snake like this one may be raised by zoologists in a museum or zoo, where it would be safe from being eaten by another animal.

13

THE SNAKE'S BODY

*S*nakes come in many different shapes. Their heads may be round, diamond-shaped, or even blunt like a sausage. Their bodies may be long and slender or thick and squat, or anywhere in between. Their tails may be pointed, flat, or round and shaped like their heads.

By David T. Roberts, Courtesy of Dallas Zoo

◀ Tree snakes, like this Emerald Tree Boa, are often very brightly colored to match the leaves and plants.

By Jeffrey M. Howland

◀ Garter Snakes are long, slender, fast and "wiggly."

By Jeffrey M. Howland

◀ Tree snakes, like this Garden Tree Boa, hang from branches in plantations, gardens and forests.

▶ Snakes that burrow, like this Longnose Snake, often have specially shaped heads to help them dig.

By Donald Hamper

14

By David T. Roberts, Courtesy of Dallas Zoo

Why does a snake have scales?

Scales are actually a part of the snake's skin. Some snakes have rough and tough scales to protect them from getting hurt by rocks and cactus and other objects as they crawl around. Some snakes have smooth, silky scales to help them glide through dirt and leaves.

By David T. Roberts, Courtesy of Dallas Zoo

▲ This Palm Viper has brilliantly colored scales over its entire body.

▲ The scales of this Eyelash Viper are hard enough to protect it, but soft enough so that the snake can move.

◄ Scales help protect snakes from injury in harsh weather and on hard surfaces. The scales of this Eyelash Viper are colored to help it blend in.

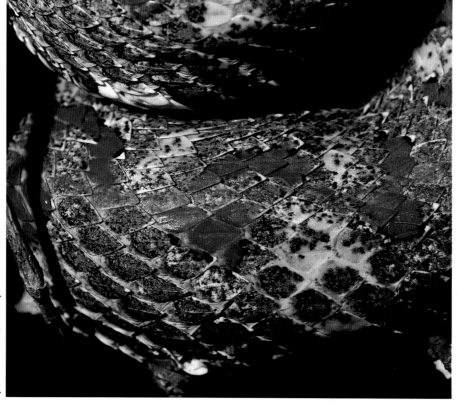

By James F. Brown, Courtesy of Fort Worth Zoo

Why are the scales so many different colors?

The scales are colored to help the snake blend in with leaves, bushes, and dirt, so his enemies can't find him easily. The pattern of the colors also helps the snake to blend in. Herpetologists use the pattern and colors of the scales to identify the snake they're looking at. They describe the patterns as banded, blotched, spotted, speckled, striped, saddled—or just say that the snake is patternless.

By Jeffrey M. Howland

▲ This Long-Nosed Snake has a "banded" pattern.

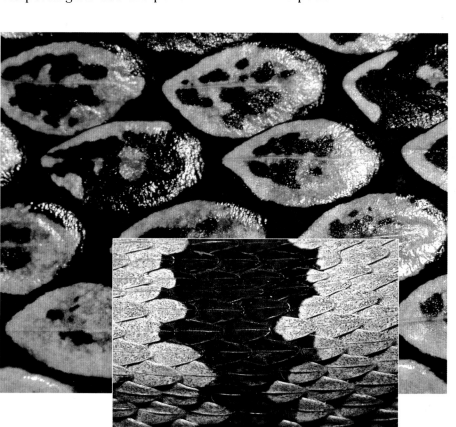

By David T. Roberts, Courtesy of Dallas Zoo

By David T. Roberts, Courtesy of Dallas Zoo

▲ Each scale on this Palm Viper has speckles, which make up its overall color pattern.

By David T. Roberts, Courtesy of Dallas Zoo

▲ This Patchnose Snake has a distinct, striped pattern.

◄ This Banded Rock Rattlesnake has bands of brown intermixed with a speckled grey that resembles the color of rocks.

17

◄ This Gaboon Viper has recently shed its skin. You can see the discarded skin lying next to it.

▼ Rainbow Boas are well known for their glossy, shiny skin and bright coloring.

▼ Snakes that have iridescent (shiny) skin, such as this D'Albert's Water Python, also have very smooth, silky-feeling scales.

By James F. Brown, Courtesy of Fort Worth Zoo

By Alan Zulich

By David T. Roberts, Courtesy of Donald M. Boyer

Why do snakes shed their skins?

Snakes have muscles, bones and organs with scales on the outside like a container. When the insides grow, the scales must stretch—but they can stretch only so much. So, when snakes outgrow their skins or injure them, they make new ones.

18

How does a snake shed its skin?

First, the new skin begins to develop under the old one. The old skin starts to get dull in color—even the eyecaps over the eyes get dull! The snake can't see during this time, and will hide and lie very still so the new skin won't be hurt. After a week or two, the snake begins to shed by pushing its nose against something rough. The skin then peels off backwards and inside out. The snake actually crawls out of its own skin!

By Roberta A. Kayne, Courtesy of Seattle Zoo

By Thomas Wright

▲ Snakes like this Cape Cobra cannot see when their eyes cloud over prior to shedding. They will be very defensive if you approach them at this time.

◀ This Trans-Pecos Rat Snake is nearly ready to shed its skin. That's why its eyes and scales are dull in color.

By Thomas Wright

►Many snakes, like this Northern Pine Snake, have larger scales on their heads than on their bodies.

▼This Horned Desert Viper gets its name from the large scales on its head that look like horns.

Why are some of the scales small and some large?

The large scales are usually on the bottom side of the snake. They help it to move more easily along the ground. Most of the time the scales overlap each other. The smaller ones are on top to help protect the skin and muscles from the heat of the sun.

By David T. Roberts, Courtesy of Dallas Zoo

What is the large scale on the bottom near the tail?

That scale is called the Anal Plate. It covers the opening through which the snake reproduces and expels its wastes. From that scale to the end of the snake is the *tail*.

By James F. Brown, Courtesy of Dallas Zoo

◄ Rhinoceros Vipers have large scales that form horns on their nose.

Are the scales waterproof?

Not really. A snake is able to absorb water from between the scales. Some snakes actually get a portion of the water they need through their skin, so they don't have to drink very much. In a place that is humid and rainy but doesn't have many puddles or ponds, this really helps the snake to survive.

By James F. Brown, Courtesy of Dallas Zoo

By David T. Roberts, Courtesy of Dallas Zoo

◄ Many snakes, such as this Green Tree Python, absorb small amounts of water from their scales.

▲ The Many-Horned Adder has small horns over its eyes that look like eyebrows or eyelashes.

21

By Jeffrey M. Howland

◄ This Black-Headed Snake is one of the smallest snakes. Most small snakes are also very slender.

▼ With its long, narrow head and extremely slender body, this Vine Snake is one of the strangest-looking creatures in the world.

What is underneath all those scales?

First, there is the skin, and then there are muscles. The bigger snakes have very large, strong muscles that they use to hold onto tree branches, for example. Under the muscles are the snakes' insides—their stomachs, hearts, lungs, and so on. The snake has the same organs as other animals, but they are placed in different ways. Finally, snakes have hundreds of bones that make up their backs. These bones are specially made to let the snake move every which way—backwards, forwards, and even upside down!

By Jeffrey M. Howland

▲ This Vine Snake has a narrow, peculiar head. It has a very slender body as well.

By David T. Roberts, Courtesy of Dallas Zoo

How do the snake's bones work?

The bones in the snake's back are called vertebrae, and a pair of ribs is attached to each one. The bones fit together smoothly so the snake is able to bend in many directions.

▶ **This Cobra skull is made up of small, delicate bones. If the bones were big, the snake wouldn't be able to move.**

By Donald Hamper

By Donald Hamper

▲ **This Palestine Viper has a stout, heavy body and large muscles. Heavy snakes usually move more slowly than slender snakes.**

How do the snake's muscles work?

A snake's muscles are very complicated. They expand and contract along the sides of the snake's body to help push it along. A snake also has muscles in its head and neck that are used in eating.

How exactly does a snake get around?

It crawls on its belly, which has larger, flatter scales that stretch and move in a pattern to pull the snake forward or back. Have you ever seen a caterpillar crawl? Well, some snakes crawl like that—bunching up some of their muscles and arching their backs while they advance in a straight line. Others do what we call the "serpentine wriggle" by moving in S-curves. They use rocks and ridges in the ground to help them.

▲ Sidewinders are named for the unusual way that they crawl.

Are there other ways that snakes move?

Several. The "sidewinder" motion that some snakes use is very strange-looking. The snake throws the middle of its body to the side and forward, but it keeps its head and neck raised above the ground. It then makes a little twist with its body and pushes itself forward. One kind of snake is called a Sidewinder because of this peculiar way of moving.

▲ Most snakes, such as this Ringed Brown Snake, move in S-curves.

Can snakes swim?

Most snakes can, but Sea Snakes and Water Snakes often also glide along by using water currents.

▶When frightened, Water Snakes will lunge into the water to get away from their enemies.

By Jeffrey M. Howland

By Jeffrey M. Howland

Can snakes climb trees?

Most snake species can climb very well—even on trees without many branches—because they have special scales along the bottom that grip the tree bark.

◀Many tree snakes, such as this Garden Tree Boa, live most of their lives hanging from tree branches.

25

▶This Ford's Boa has twisted himself up so that he looks as if he's tied in a knot.

By Thomas Wright

By James F. Brown, Courtesy of Fort Worth Zoo

Can a snake tie itself in a knot?

No, they are not quite that flexible. They can wrap their coils around each other several times, though, so they end up *looking* as if they are coiled in knots.

▲ Some snakes, like this Louisiana Pine Snake, are good at burrowing into holes in the ground.

▼ The Patchnose Snake is named for the large scale covering the end of its nose.

Can a snake dig, or does it have to find a hole to hide in?

Some snakes take advantage of a hole dug by another animal and use it to hide in, but many snakes actually burrow and dig their own holes. These snakes have more rounded heads. Some have special noses that allow them to dig in the dirt.

By David T. Roberts, Courtesy of Dallas Zoo

26

Can a snake push or pull with its body?

You bet it can! A snake is especially good at pushing leaves, sticks, and small rocks around, and it can even push open doors, if it's big enough. However, most snakes tend to crawl *around* the obstacle, such as through the crack under the door, because it takes a lot of energy to push things out of the way.

By Thomas Wright

◄ A Jamaican Boa has a "prehensile" tail that can support its entire weight.

▼ This Black-Necked Spitting Cobra warns off its enemies by standing up and spreading its hood.

How are snakes able to raise their body off the ground?

Snakes' muscles are very strong. They tense up these muscles to raise their heads off the ground. Some snakes have such strong muscles that they can raise much of their body off the ground and into the air. They look almost as if they're standing.

Another amazing feat of strength: Some snakes can dangle the entire weight of their body just from their tail. That's because they have a prehensile tail—one that is able to grab and hold onto things.

By Donald Hamper

THE SNAKE'S SENSES

Well, a snake's body is pretty strange, and how it works is just as strange! Imagine what it would be like to smell with your tongue and hear with your body—because that is exactly what a snake does!

By Jeffrey M. Howland

◄ This Rosy Boa, like all snakes, uses its body and tongue to find food. It can even hunt in the dark.

By Donald Hamper

◄ Venomous Snakes, like this Cottonmouth, are able to locate warm, living animals very quickly.

By James F. Brown, Courtesy of Fort Worth Zoo

◄ When poisonous snakes like this Sedge Viper try to catch food, they almost never miss.

► Garter Snakes have such sensitive bodies that they can find tiny fish swimming in moving water.

By Jeffrey M. Howland

How do you know if a snake is asleep?

You don't, since its eyes never close! And, since a snake wakes up very quickly when approached, most people will never see one sleeping. Snakes can lie very still even when awake, so it is difficult to tell by just looking.

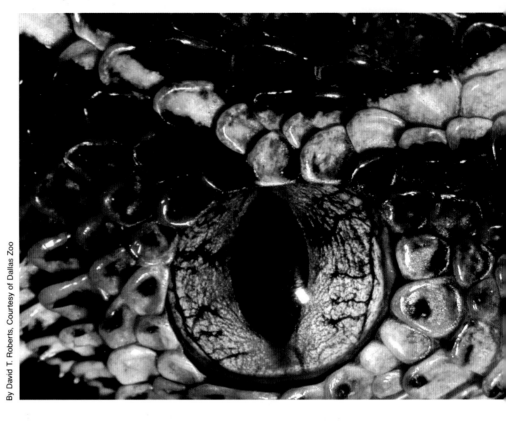

By David T. Roberts, Courtesy of Dallas Zoo

By Annette T. Wright

▲ **This Rhinoceros Viper, like all snakes, will never be able to blink. All snakes sleep with their eyes open.**

◄ **Snakes rest whenever they feel comfortable and safe. Many are more active at night.**

Why do snakes stare so much?

If you look really closely, you'll see that snakes have no eyelids, so they cannot shut their eyes. They don't need eyelids, because they have a tough scale over their eyes (like contact lenses) to protect them.

Here's a tip: If anyone ever dares you to "stare down" a snake until one of you blinks, don't fall for it!

What exactly do snakes see?

Snakes cannot see details of objects but can make out general shapes, especially of things that are close to them. The best thing about the snake's sight is that moving objects show up really well.

By David T. Roberts, Courtesy of Dallas Zoo

◀ Some snakes, like this Blunt-Headed Tree Snake, have large eyes with vertical pupils. This helps them find food in the dark.

▼ Temporarily blind, this Indigo Snake will be able to see again when its shedding is completed.

Do snakes see colors?

Yes, actually they do, but we don't know which colors they see best. One Ball Python we knew would put her head up and stretch towards anything that was colored blue, and shy away from the color red—but we were never quite sure if it was the color she liked or the object.

Can a snake be blind?

Any snake's eyes can be damaged badly enough for it to lose its sight. But all snakes actually have periods where they are considered blind—and that's when they're shedding. The scale over their eyes becomes so cloudy that they just can't see.

By Jeffrey M. Howland

By Thomas Wright

▲ Scientists have learned that snakes see color. Some snakes, like this Ball Python, even have favorite colors.

31

Do snakes have ears? If not, how do they hear?

That is the major thing that makes a snake a snake and not a lizard—it doesn't have ears. Snakes do not hear sounds through the air as we do; they feel the vibrations that moving objects or animals make on the ground and in the water. The bones in their jaws help them feel these movements, and since snakes lie directly on the ground, they can feel such movements very easily.

▲ Like all snakes, this Timber Rattlesnake is able to feel even the slightest vibration through its body.

How does a snake smell?

A snake smells with its tongue.

Inside its mouth is a special membrane called the *Jacobsen's organ*. The snake's little forked tongue flicks out of its mouth again and again, picking up tiny particles from the environment. The Jacobsen's organ analyzes them. This tells the snake where its prey is (its prey is the animal it wants to eat).

◄ All snakes, like this Pine Snake, use their tongue to smell particles in the air. That gives them a "picture" of what is around them.

► Snakes like this Ornate Cantil move their tongue rapidly in and out of their mouth—and sometimes up and down as well.

What other senses do snakes have?

Snakes can feel over every part of their body. Some of the scales are especially sensitive and help to pick up vibrations. Snakes also have the ability to detect *heat*.

You mean, they know when it's hot?

Actually, it's much more than that. Snakes have the ability to sense live prey, which they eat. Many snakes have heat sensors called *pits* along the front or sides of their jaw and nose. Inside these pits are small organs that react when a warm creature is near. Many venomous snakes have these pits—that's why they're called "Pit Vipers."

►This Emerald Tree Boa has a long row of heat pits on its head, making it a very efficient hunter of birds and small mammals.

►The openings just below and in front of this Ball Python's eyes are its heat-sensing pits.

▼ This Neotropical Rattlesnake has deep, circular heat-sensing pits. Pit Vipers use them to detect prey.

By Thomas Wright

By David T. Roberts, Courtesy of Dallas Zoo

By Roberta A. Kayne, Courtesy of Dallas Zoo

EATING HABITS

Snakes are carnivores and usually eat live prey. That includes other snakes, fish, insects, frogs, lizards, rodents such as rats and mice, and other small mammals. A few snakes eat special foods, such as eggs and snails.

By David T. Roberts, Courtesy of Dallas Zoo

◀ The Massasauga is a small species of Rattlesnake that lies in wait for its prey of frogs, lizards and mice.

By James F. Brown, Courtesy of Fort Worth Zoo

◀ Texas Ratsnakes are a favorite of farmers, since they eat large numbers of rats and mice.

By James F. Brown, Courtesy of Dallas Zoo

◀ The Horned Desert Viper lies almost completely buried in sand. When prey walks by, it takes it by surprise.

▶ Eyelash Vipers often catch their food while dangling from a branch. They may even pull it up into the tree to eat it.

By James F. Brown, Courtesy of Fort Worth Zoo

Do snakes ever eat other snakes?

Yes, some snakes eat other snakes for food. Kingsnakes especially do it—they even eat poisonous snakes.

▶ **A Speckled Kingsnake is very important, because it can kill and eat more venomous snakes, such as Rattlesnakes.**

By David T. Roberts, Courtesy of Dallas Zoo

By Jeffrey M. Howland

◀ **This is a Snail-Eating Snake from South America. The jaws of these snakes move in such a way that they can pull snails out of their shells.**

▶ **All snakes need exercise to stay in shape, especially those with thick, heavy bodies like this Blood Python.**

Will a snake eat something that is already dead?

Not usually. The problem is not that a snake doesn't like food that's been killed; it's that it can't find it. Remember, a snake sees moving objects or picks up the vibrations of moving objects, and dead things don't move.

▶ **Many fast snakes, like this Coachwhip, are able to capture and eat lizards and other quick-moving animals.**

By Jeffrey M. Howland

By Jeffrey M. Howland

By Roberta A. Kayne, Courtesy of Fort Worth Zoo

Do snakes get fat?

Yes, if for some reason snakes are able to get more food than usual, they may get too fat. This is dangerous for a snake, because a fat snake may not be able to move away from danger quickly enough.

Also, it's easy for a snake to overeat. At one meal it could eat prey that is very large compared to itself—and then be unable to move for hours or days! This is why it is not likely that even the largest snake would eat a horse or a cow or a person. If it did, it would place itself in danger.

How do snakes capture their food?

This depends on which snake you're talking about. In general, there are two ways:

1. *By using venom*. Poisonous snakes, such as Rattlesnakes, have large fangs connected to glands that are full of venom (poison). When they strike and inject the animal with venom, their prey is soon unable to move, and the snake can eat it easily. The venom also starts breaking down the food so the snake can digest it.

2. *By constriction*. Many snakes, especially Boas and Pythons, wrap their bodies tightly around their prey and squeeze tighter and tighter until the animal cannot breathe and dies.

▲ Some snakes, like this Green Vine Snake, can sneak up on their prey because they blend into their surroundings and move very quickly.

Do snakes chew their food?

No, snakes don't crush, chew, pull apart, or change their food in any way—they simply swallow it in one solid piece— even prey that is 2 to 3 times bigger than their head.

▲ Many snakes, like this Amethystine Python, are called constrictors because that is the way they kill their prey.

▶ If this Hognose Viper couldn't capture its prey using venom, it would have a hard time catching lizards, which are faster than snakes.

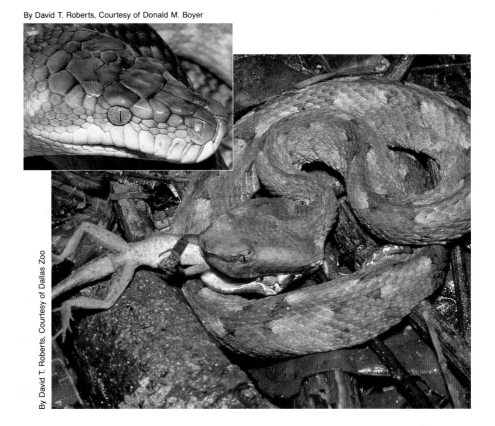

38

Do snakes ever choke on their food?

A snake's head and neck expand very, very much to allow large food items to pass through. A snake's lungs are designed so that the snake can breathe even when its throat is filled with food.

How can the snake open its mouth that wide?

The snake's jawbones are connected with stretchy muscles. The upper and lower jawbones stretch apart from each other upwards and downwards. Since the lower jawbone is not solid and in one piece like ours, it can also stretch apart from side to side, making even more room for a large food item to pass through.

▶ Snakes' jawbones are separate from each other, unlike ours, which are hinged together. That is why this Albino Corn Snake can eat large prey without any problems.

By Thomas Wright

▲ This Burmese Python is going through the process of eating its prey. Its mouth can actually open even wider than this.

By Annette Wright

Do snakes yawn?

Yes, snakes do it sometimes to get their jaws in line so they can be more comfortable. You see it often when a snake is finished eating—it's almost as if it has to put its jaw back together after it eats.

Do snakes have teeth?

Yes, all snakes have small teeth that are curved like hooks. They help to snag the food and pull it into the snake's mouth and throat. Venomous snakes have fangs as well as teeth and the fangs are much larger. Some snakes have fangs in the front of their mouth, and some in the back.

What are the fangs for?

The fangs of venomous snakes are connected to glands full of poison. The fangs act like needles that inject venom into the prey.

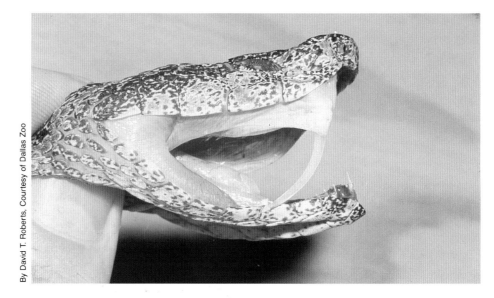

▲ (Above) You can see the fangs of this Broad-Banded Copperhead clearly. Fangs are hollow, and venom flows through them into the snakes' prey.

▲ (Below) Fangs of venomous snakes, like this Speckled Forest Pit Viper, are very sharp, like the needle the doctor uses when you get a shot.

What is the difference between venom and saliva?

Both saliva and venom play a role in eating. Venom is made up of chemicals that poison the prey, preventing it from moving. Sometimes it actually kills the animal before the snake eats it. Some snake venom begins digesting the food before it reaches the stomach.

The main action of saliva is to help slide the food from the mouth into the throat. The saliva of some snakes may also digest the food a bit, but it's not the same as venom.

By James F. Brown, Courtesy of Fort Worth Zoo

By Jeffrey M. Howland

▲ The fangs of most Vipers, such as this McGregor's Pit Viper, fold into the roof of the mouth when not being used. It is these fangs and venom glands that give Vipers their large heads.

◄ Some snakes like this Parrot Snake use a very mild venom on the small prey that they eat. They inject it through fangs located way in the back of their mouth.

41

Do snakes drink?

Yes, snakes drink from puddles and other pools of water. Some drink drops of water off leaves and even off their own bodies. They usually use their mouths to drink, but some snakes absorb water through their skin when it gets wet.

By David T. Roberts, Courtesy Dallas Zoo

▲ Some snakes, like this Two-Lined Viper, allow raindrops or dew to collect on their body, and then drink it.

▼ After snakes finish eating, they stretch and squirm to help the food get into their stomach—and sometimes they even yawn!

By Thomas Wright

How does the food get digested?

Strong muscles in a snake's neck and body produce "waves" that move the food along. Some snakes also use gravity to help the food along, by holding their heads in the air so the food flows down. Then it goes into the stomach and intestines—one long, stretchy tube inside the body.

Do snakes ever throw up?

Yes, if the snake is stressed out after eating, or frightened, or if it's too hot or cold, or if its food doesn't pass into its stomach, the "waves" that the muscles make can go in the opposite direction. Snakes usually rest for several hours or even days after they eat to keep this from happening.

By Roberta A. Kayne, Courtesy of Fort Worth Zoo

▲ Those snakes that eat often, like Black Pine Snakes, have a tendency to eat a lot at one time. They may throw up some of the food if they have to move quickly after eating.

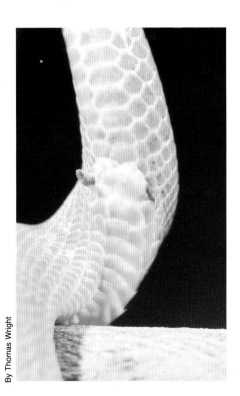

By Thomas Wright

What do wastes look like?

Most of the waste is brown or black, as with most animals. Snake urine, though, is white or yellow and "sandy." It is also solid, rather than liquid as with most other animals.

◄ All snakes, like this young Green Tree Python, have an opening called the cloaca at the end of the body, through which wastes pass. The rest is the tail.

How do snakes pass wastes?

Most everything gets digested when a snake eats, but the snake may get rid of some bits of fur and other parts several days after eating through the opening called the cloaca at the end of the body.

SNAKE REPRODUCTION

There are 3 ways to tell male snakes from female snakes. Male snakes sometimes have longer tails.

Males have hemipenes *in* their tail. Females don't.

Boas and Pythons often have small, bony lumps called "spurs" near their tail.

By Jeffrey M. Howland

◄ All Rattlesnakes, like this Sidewinder, give live birth to many babies at a time.

By Jeffrey M. Howland

◄ Baby Whipsnakes look just like their parents, only much smaller.

By Roberta A. Kayne, Courtesy of Fort Worth Zoo

◄ Adult Wagler's Pit Vipers are less colorful than their young.

► Tree snakes, like the Ceylonese Tree Viper, live in trees, but usually have their babies on the ground.

By James F. Brown, Courtesy of Fort Worth Zoo

What are "spurs"?

Millions of years ago, the snakes we know today had legs. Spurs are the remains of the hip bones they once had. Male Boas and Pythons have larger, longer and more pointed spurs. Females usually have smaller, rounded ones.

►The spurs of this young male Green Tree Python are very long and hard. He uses them to stroke the female during courtship.

By Thomas Wright

By Tom Wright

How do hemipenes work?

Hemipenes are small organs in the lower part of the male snake's tail that are used for mating. The sperm cells, which mix with the female's eggs to produce offspring, need a way to get into the female. The hemipenes provide that connection during mating.

◄ It is difficult to tell a female from a male, even if the snake is large, like this Yellow Anaconda.

46

Why don't all snakes have spurs?

Over many thousands of years, the bodies of snakes have changed at different rates of speed. Spurs disappeared in many of the snake species, but Boas and Pythons, who have not changed as much, still have them.

Why do male snakes have longer tails than females?

When they are not being used, the hemipenes nestle inside an opening in the tail. This protects them from injury. Since the hemipenes can sometimes be pretty long, the tail is usually long also.

▶Venomous snakes like this Eyelash Viper have not been in existence as long as Boas and Pythons and do not have spurs.

▶Sometimes male snakes are more brightly colored than females, which can help in telling them apart.

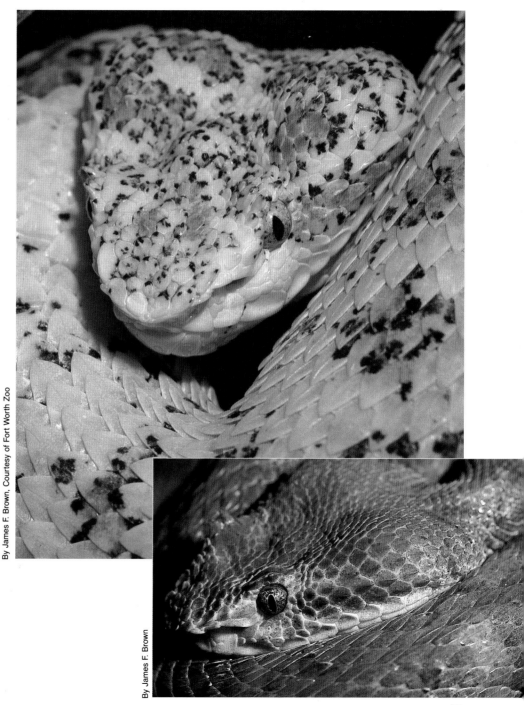

By James F. Brown, Courtesy of Fort Worth Zoo

By James F. Brown

47

What do male and female snakes do to attract each other?

Each species of snake, as well as each individual, has its own mechanisms for attracting the opposite sex. Some do complex dances and fancy movements, while others spray a scent to attract other snakes.

We don't know for sure what qualities a snake looks for when choosing a mate, but it's easy to see that a lot of "body language" goes on during courting.

▼ **Some snakes like this Southern Pine Snake may twitch again and again to attract a mate during courtship.**

By Jeffrey M. Howland

Will two males fight for a female?

Yes, two males often compete over a female. This can look very much like a dance—they weave around each other, hissing or striking out. But, the snakes seldom get hurt, and the loser ends up crawling away.

How do snakes mate?

During the courting stage, the snakes often rub against each other. Then, their tails intertwine as the male quickly inserts one of his hemipenes into the female. They may stay intertwined for several hours—even up to a whole day. Occasionally, they will mate again later or on another day.

By James F. Brown, Courtesy of Fort Worth Zoo

▲ Once these Black-Tailed Vipers are finished mating, they will go their separate ways.

▶ These Aruba Island Rattlesnakes are heavily involved in mating. It would take a lot to make them separate from each other.

By David T. Roberts, Courtesy of Dallas Zoo

▼ The courtship movements of Milksnakes look like a fancy dance and are very elaborate.

How can the male hold onto the female for so long?

Some male snakes have spurs, remember, that they use to latch onto the females. Some males have spines on their hemipenes that lock into the female so they can't be separated easily. Also, many snakes wrap snugly around each other in order to stay put.

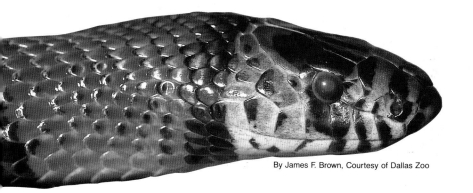

By James F. Brown, Courtesy of Dallas Zoo

Do the two snakes stay together as a couple?

Not in most cases. Once the female is pregnant, she usually doesn't want to be with the male and will sometimes even fight with him. However, the King Cobra is one species in which both male and female guard the eggs until they hatch.

How can you tell that a snake is pregnant?

At the beginning of a pregnancy, it's hard to tell. Later on, the last third of the snake's body and the tail get very rounded-looking. Some snakes lay eggs, and you can sometimes make out their outline within the mother's body.

How do baby snakes grow?

There are two ways: Some baby snakes grow inside the mother for the entire time, and then, when they are big

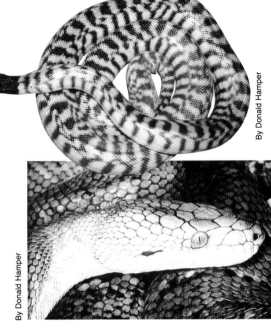

► The main difference between Boas and Pythons is that Pythons (above) lay eggs and Boas (below) have their babies live.

enough, are born. This is called *live birth*, and it is a lot like what mammals do.

The other way that baby snakes grow is inside an egg. These snakes, called *egg layers*, lay the eggs, which hatch after a short time.

By Donald Hamper

By David T. Roberts, Courtesy of Dallas Zoo

▲ Baby snakes from mothers who give live birth, like this Neotropical Rattlesnake, are born in clear sacs filled with liquid.

50

By Jeffrey M. Howland

◄ The Bushmaster is the only viper in the tropical areas of South and Central America that lays eggs. The others give live birth.

▼ Eggs come in different shapes and sizes. Female snakes can lay small or large numbers of eggs, depending on the species.

Are all eggs alike?

No, just like snakes, eggs come in many shapes and sizes. Some eggs are round or oval, and some are longer than they are wide, looking like sausages. Small snakes may lay very large eggs, and some eggs are as tiny as a grain of rice.

By Donald Hamper

How long does it take for the babies to be born?

A live birth usually takes 4–8 months from the time the mother becomes pregnant to the time of the birth.

With egg layers, it usually takes about 2–4 months from becoming pregnant to laying the eggs. Then the eggs take anywhere from one to 3 months to hatch.

51

Where do snakes have babies?

Pregnant snakes try to find a safe place to hide and stay warm when they give birth or lay eggs. Remember, they get very heavy and can't move around much when full of babies, and need a place to hide to stay safe. Sometimes a female snake will nestle into piles of leaves, sand, or other material and move around to mold a kind of "nest" for herself and her babies or eggs.

How many babies do female snakes have?

It depends on the species, but females can either lay or give birth to anywhere from 2 to 100 babies at a time.

Does a female stay with her eggs?

Some snakes will lay eggs in a warm hidden area, sometimes even partly burying them, and then leave the eggs to hatch on their own. Sometimes they will stay nearby to protect them, but often they just leave. Pythons are unique in that they wrap themselves around their eggs and warm them while they develop.

By Donald Hamper

◄ This female snake, a Ramsay's Python, is protecting her eggs with her body coils while she warms them.

By Roberta A. Kayne, Courtesy of Dallas Zoo

By Roberta A. Kayne

▲ Eggs can get damaged, wet or even eaten by another animal. These Diamond Pythons, like most female Pythons, coil around their eggs and keep them warm.

If snakes are cold-blooded, how can they warm their eggs?

Great question! There is one exception to the term cold-blooded. (Remember, that means the snake gets its warmth from the air and ground around it.) A Python female is able to raise her body temperature—but only to warm the eggs. She does it by twitching and moving her body around.

Can eggs break?

Well, they can, but it doesn't happen often. The shells of snake eggs are not hard and brittle like birds' eggs. They are made of a tough, leathery material that is rather soft and can stretch a little. The eggs can tear open, but they usually don't, because they are protected by being partially buried, in a secure nest or by their mother's body.

By Donald Hamper

◄ This Ramsay's Python, will surround her eggs with her body loosely if they're warm or more closely if they're cold.

By James F. Brown, Courtesy of Fort Worth Zoo

▲ Most snakes, including this Mexican Lancehead Rattlesnake, will move to a sheltered area to give birth or lay their eggs.

Are the eggs waterproof?

No, and this is another good reason for a female snake to find a hiding place for them. Water can get through the leathery shell. The eggs need some water, but too much of it will cause the babies to die while inside the eggs.

The baby snakes also breathe air that flows through the outer shell. Females never completely bury the eggs. If they did, the babies would suffocate.

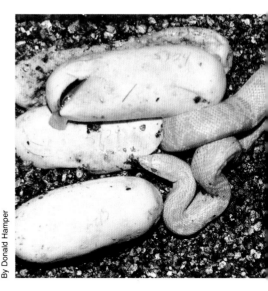

▲ When this Albino Pine Snake was still inside its egg, it had an umbilical cord attached to a yolk that nourished it.

▲ Being a desert animal, this Speckled Rattlesnake must hunt at night when it's cool. Only those that are strong enough to find food will survive.

How do the babies get food?

Babies that are born live get food and water from their mother's body. The babies in eggs have yolk and fluid inside the egg that help them to grow, as well as water from the environment.

After the babies are born, they must fend for themselves, because the mother doesn't take care of them.

How do baby snakes get out of their eggs?

Baby snakes have a hard sort of tooth on the top side of their nose area. It's called an *egg tooth*, and they use it to rip open their shells. Snakes that are born live also have this tooth. They are born in a clear bag that is full of liquid, and they have to open it themselves after they are born. The egg tooth falls off after a few days.

How long does it take a baby snake to hatch?

It takes several days from start to finish. Once the baby snake gets its head out, it usually looks around while it takes a rest. Is it waiting to see if it's safe? We don't know, but eventually the baby snake wiggles out of the egg.

By David T. Roberts, Courtesy of Dallas Zoo

▲ This newborn snake, a Pueblan Milksnake, cut open its leathery shell, and is now hatching.

▼ This newborn Bushmaster is cautiously looking around before coming out of its egg.

By David T. Roberts, Courtesy of Dallas Zoo

How do babies learn to catch food?

First of all, baby snakes don't need to eat right away—the food they got from their mother or from the yolk of the egg keeps them healthy for several weeks.

Second, they don't need to learn how to eat; they know how by instinct without being taught. The problem is finding food. Baby snakes are extremely small, usually 4 to 12 inches, depending upon the kind of snake. They may have a hard time finding food small enough to eat.

By Roberta A. Kayne, Courtesy of Fort Worth Zoo

By James F. Brown, Courtesy of Fort Worth Zoo

▲ Adult Guatamalan Tree Vipers live high in the trees. Their babies live in the lower branches. This way the babies can get food more easily.

◄ A number of baby snakes, including the Cottonmouth, are born with colored tail tips that they wiggle to attract frogs and lizards so they can eat.

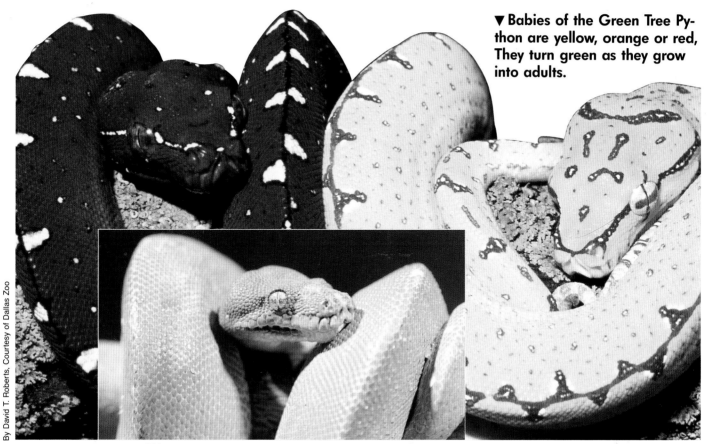

By David T. Roberts, Courtesy of Dallas Zoo

By Thomas Wright

▼ Babies of the Green Tree Python are yellow, orange or red, They turn green as they grow into adults.

Do baby snakes look like adult snakes?

Most baby snakes are brighter in color than adult snakes, and, of course, they are much smaller. Some species are a completely different color when they are babies, and they change to the usual adult color as they grow.

▲ Young Green Tree Pythons, like many other snakes, have a different color or pattern from their parents.

▶ Some baby snakes, like this Ringed Python, have different patterns from the adult. This snake is losing its rings as it gets older. It doesn't have many left.

By Donald Hamper

57

SELF-DEFENSE

Snakes bite if they are afraid. If they have tried to escape or warn off an enemy, and it hasn't worked, they bite to defend themselves.

By Jeffrey M. Howland

◄ The Mussurana is a very useful snake, since it eats venomous snakes. It will also eat non-venomous snakes.

By Roberta A. Kayne, Courtesy of Seattle Zoo

◄ Giant snakes, like the Reticulated Python, have only a few enemies they must protect themselves from. One of them is humankind.

By Donald Hamper

◄ A Death Adder will flatten its head, hiss, and puff up its body to warn an enemy to "stay away."

► When captured, Garter Snakes sometimes release smelly liquid from their tail. This is called "musk."

By Jeffrey M. Howland

How do snakes bite?

When capturing food, snakes bite and hold on in most cases.

A snake that bites when it's frightened, bites rapidly without holding on. This is called *striking*, and they often do it over and over. Most of the time, the snake doesn't even aim its strikes, but just darts out into the general direction of the enemy.

Do snakes bite right away when they are frightened?

If a snake is startled—especially if it's startled while mating, having babies, or shedding—it may strike immediately. Usually, though, most snakes first try to escape or hide from their enemy. If that doesn't work, they will try to scare the enemy off by hissing or giving some kind of obvious warning. Striking and biting are used as a last resort.

By James F. Brown, Courtesy of Dallas Zoo

By Thomas Wright

▲ This Uracoan Rattlesnake is preparing to defend itself. You can see the rattles on its tail.

◄ This Puerto Rican Boa is trying to bite to defend itself, because it is afraid.

What else do snakes do to protect themselves?

Most snakes are able to rapidly and silently move away from danger. If not, they simply lie very still so that no one will see them. Snakes hiss loudly, rattle their tails, or even blow themselves up to look bigger than they are, to scare their enemies. Some snakes roll into a tight ball when they are frightened. Some will even roll over and "play dead" or release smelly liquid from their body if they are badly frightened.

By Jeffrey M. Howland

▲ Some snakes, like this Night Snake, roll themselves tightly into a coil to protect themselves.

◄ With its shaggy scales and combination of yellow, green and brown colors, this Rough-Scaled Tree Viper is very hard to spot in the forest where it lives.

By James F. Brown, Courtesy of Dallas Zoo

By David T. Roberts, Courtesy of Dallas Zoo

◄ Hognose snakes play dead to defend themselves. If you turn them right side up, they'll flip back over as if to prove they are really dead!

► Some snakes, like this Ring-neck Snake, have brightly colored undersides that they display when defending themselves.

By Jeffrey M. Howland

61

How does the musk spray work?

Any animal that is able to smell would probably be turned away by the terrible smell that some snakes produce. Humans, especially, back off very quickly from this very bad odor! The musk is a chemical released from glands in the tail, and it is so repulsive that most people run quickly for soap and water if it gets on their skin.

How do Rattlesnakes rattle?

Rattlesnakes have hollow, over-lapping scales on the tips of their tails. When they are irritated, they vibrate these scales, making a very loud buzzing noise to scare off their enemy.

By David T. Roberts, Courtesy of Dallas Zoo

By Thomas Wright

▲ Rattlesnakes get a new button on their rattle each time they shed.

◄ The rattles of this Black-Tailed Rattlesnake are hollow and make a loud buzzing sound when the snake vibrates them.

What snakes make themselves look bigger?

Cobras are famous for doing it. They raise themselves far off the ground and stretch out their hood—the skin that surrounds their head. This makes them look much larger, and might possibly make another animal think twice about attacking them.

How do snakes hiss?

Snakes hiss by breathing out air through their nose. This makes a loud "woosh" sound. Many snakes store air in their body. When they are startled, they exhale it very loudly and for a long time.

▶ **Some snakes, like this Bull-snake, hiss very loudly by forcing air out of their windpipes.**

By Jeffrey M. Howland

▲ **Puffing Snakes inflate their throats, flatten their bodies, and "puff themselves up" when defending themselves.**

▶ **This Albino Cobra is spreading the scales around its head to form a hood, which makes it look larger.**

By Donald Hamper

By David T. Roberts, Courtesy of Dallas Zoo

63

How do you tell a poisonous snake from one that is not?

Some scientists say they can identify a venomous snake by the shape of its head. Some snakes have triangular-shaped heads, and many of those are poisonous. But the only way they can tell for sure is to see the fangs. And, it is never safe to try to open a snake's mouth!

By David T. Roberts, Courtesy of Dallas Zoo

◀ Some Coral Snakes can be identified by the pattern of their rings. For example, here the red rings always touch the yellow rings.

▼ Milksnakes are not venomous, but are often mistaken for Coral Snakes, which are.

By Roberta A. Kayne, Courtesy of Dallas Zoo

When a poisonous snake bites, does it always inject venom?

The only way a snake can inject venom into another animal is for its fangs to actually break the skin. Often, poisonous snakes strike or bite or even use their fangs, but don't break the skin. The snake doesn't inject venom on purpose; it just happens automatically when the fangs are released and plunged in. Remember that, if you are bitten by a snake that is poisonous—or if you are not sure whether it's poisonous—*you must always go to the hospital for treatment.*

▶ Even though this Albino Diamondback Rattlesnake has rattles and venom—like all Rattlesnakes—its color is so light that a bird or other animal would be able to catch it very easily.

By David T. Roberts, Courtesy of Dallas Zoo

▲ Some venomous snakes, like this Terciopelo, have large, flat heads because of the fangs and venom glands folded inside.

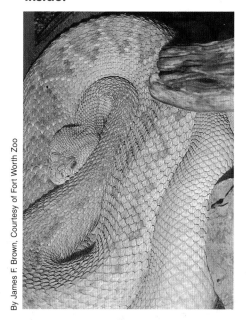

By James F. Brown, Courtesy of Fort Worth Zoo

By Thomas Wright

▲ This Pacific Boa is not venomous, but it has a flat triangular head. It is sometimes called a Viper Boa for that reason.

SNAKES AND PEOPLE

Snakes are useful to us— they eat the rats, mice and insects that can cause diseases. Some snakes eat other snakes, keeping everything in balance. If we start killing many of one kind of creature, nature will get all messed up.

By Jeffrey M. Howland

◀ Coral Snakes are poisonous, but they are small and shy. If left alone, they aren't as deadly as most people think.

By James F. Brown, Courtesy of Fort Worth Zoo

◀ Copperheads are venomous, but are useful to us because their venom goes into the medicine that treats snakebite.

By David T. Roberts , Courtesy of Dallas Zoo

◀ Various cultures, including some Native American tribes, have worshiped and protected snakes like the Massasauga.

▶ Whipsnakes are common and found in many parts of the world.

By Jeffrey M. Howland

66

Which snakes get along best with people?

Many Albino snakes, such as Albino Kingsnakes, may be safer with people than in the wild, where they would not live very long. Other snakes that seem to get along with people are Corn Snakes and Milk Snakes.

Can a snake's fangs be removed so it's not poisonous?

No, this would not work. Poisonous snakes have several sets of fangs. If you remove one set, another is right behind it. Even if you were to remove all of them, its teeth and fangs would grow back very quickly. Some people have tried to squeeze or "milk" the venom out of the snake, but the snake just makes more. "Milking" itself is very dangerous!

By James F. Brown, Courtesy of Fort Worth Zoo

▲ In some areas of the United States, it is said that farmers put Corn Snakes in their cornfields to eat mice and rats.

▶ Kingsnakes are common, very useful snakes. But an albino like this cannot hide from its enemies well. It would probably be eaten if it was in the wild.

By Donald Hamper

◀ Milksnakes got their name because people believed that they lived in barns and took milk from cows. They are found frequently in barns, but actually eat rats and mice.

By David T. Roberts, Courtesy of Dallas Zoo

What can I do to protect myself from getting bitten?

The best way is to understand that snakes only bite people when they are frightened—and to make sure that you don't frighten them. If you see a snake, walk around it or stand still and let it crawl away from you. If a snake does try to bite, don't beat on it or step on it—that only upsets it more. Stand still, let it calm down on its own, and then let it crawl away.

By David T. Roberts, Courtesy of Dallas Zoo

By James F. Brown, Courtesy of Fort Worth Zoo

▲ This Copperhead Snake is very beautiful, but it is also very poisonous and could be deadly.

▶ Most snakes, especially small ones like these Ground Snakes, will quickly crawl away from you.

Why are some snakes hunted and killed?

In some parts of the world, snakes are hunted for food. Unfortunately, some hunters also hunt them for their skins or for sport. There are still some groups of people who enjoy killing animals for exercise and recreation, or to put their rattles or heads on display.

Why are some snakes so very rare?

Quite a few kinds of snake are rarely seen because there are so few left in the wild. Many of them are dying off because buildings and roads are destroying their homes. If this continues, several kinds of snake may become extinct, which means that they will *never* be seen again.

By Jeffrey M. Howland

▼ Some species, like this Boelen's Python, are rarely seen in the wild. They are seldom kept even by herpetologists and zoos.

▲ The Fer-de-Lance, a dangerous viper, is important to us because anti-venom to treat snakebite is made from its venom, along with venom from other snakes.

By Donald Hamper

70

What does endangered species mean?

An endangered species is an animal that may die off completely if we don't protect it. Most governments today try to protect these animals by making it illegal to capture them. There are also many other animals that are called *protected*, because they might become endangered one day if too many are taken from the wild.

What can I do to protect snakes?

Learn about snakes and teach others what you learn. You may want to teach them not to be afraid—not to kill snakes or any other wild animals. Most important of all, you might teach them not to catch wild snakes and make them into pets. Snakes are not happy in captivity, and will not be good pets.

By Donald Hamper

◄ Many governments are protective of their native creatures. This Green Tree Python is a very rare *blue* individual, native to New Guinea and Australia.

▼ When hiking in the desert or forest, bring a camera so you can take pictures of snakes—like this pretty Durango Mountain Kingsnake—if you happen to see one.

By Joe Pierce

71

GREAT SNAKES

What is a Family, a Genus and a Species of snake?

A Family is a group of snakes that share similar features. A Genus is a smaller group in the same family. A Species is a specific kind of snake. There may be many genera (more than one genus) in a family, and also many different species in a genus.

For example:

A **family** of snakes is BOIDAE.
A **genus** of Boidae is PYTHON.
A **species** of Python is BALL PYTHON.

A **family** of snakes is ELAPIDAE.
A **genus** of Elapidae is COBRA.
A **species** of Cobra is KING COBRA.

By Roberta A. Kayne, Courtesy of Dallas Zoo

▲ There are many different kinds of Boa. This Emerald Tree Boa is just one species.

How are snakes named?

Scientists called *taxonomists* help to identify animals and to name them. The names that are given to snakes sometimes tell what color they are or where they are from. Snakes have two names—*common names* that are easy to remember, but can change from country to country—and *scientific names* that are mostly used by scientists, and don't change very often.

For example: A famous species of snake that lives in Australia and New Guinea has the common name of Green Tree Python. But in some countries, it is called a Tree Python or a Green Python.

Its scientific name is *Chondropython viridis*, and that is the same all around the world.

▶ Some snakes, like this Madagascan Ground Boa, are named for the country they come from. This snake is from the island of Madagascar.

▶ The common names of many snakes, like this Ringed Python, describe their color or special features they may have.

▼ This snake has not been given a common name yet, but it has a scientific name: *Nothopsis rugosa*.

By David T. Roberts, Courtesy of Dallas Zoo

By David T. Roberts, Courtesy of Dallas Zoo

By James F. Brown, Courtesy of Fort Worth Zoo

What are the smallest snakes in the world?

There are a few snakes, called Thread Snakes, that grow to only 8 inches long. Their relatives, the Blind Snakes, are also very small.

What are the largest snakes in the world?

The Green Anaconda, a kind of Boa, is the heaviest snake in the world. The Reticulated Python is the longest snake in the world.

By Jeffrey M. Howland

▲ The Green Anaconda lives in the tropical jungles of South America near streams and swamps.

▶ "Reticulated" means: "having crossing lines," which exactly describes the color pattern of Reticulated Pythons.

74

By Roberta A. Kayne, Courtesy of Dallas Zoo

By David T. Roberts, Courtesy of Dallas Zoo

▲ One of the smallest Pythons is the Angolan Python, found in Africa.

◀ Blind Snakes have a scale that covers their small eyes so that it looks as if they have no eyes at all.

By Roberta A. Kayne, Courtesy of Seattle Zoo

What are the fastest snakes?

Whipsnakes and Racers are kinds of snakes that move very fast. The Coachwhip and the Indigo Snake are two of the fastest kinds of snake.

By Donald Hamper

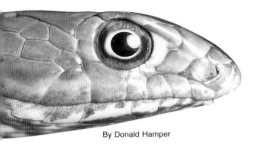
By Donald Hamper

▲ People used to believe that Coachwhips would "whip" their prey to death. We know now that this is only a myth.

▲ Indigo Snakes are able to eat venomous snakes, and they are also one of the few species that eat turtles.

▼ Death Adders raise their tails and wave them slightly as a lure to attract their prey.

What are the slowest snakes?

(The ones that are asleep!) Actually, some snakes, like the Death Adder, move very little and lie in wait for their prey. Many large snakes have heavy bodies and move quite slowly.

By David T. Roberts, Courtesy of Dallas Zoo

Which snakes are the most dangerous?

All venomous snakes are dangerous if you're bitten by one. The Mamba and the Coral Snake are two of many venomous snakes.

◄Green Mambas are large, venomous snakes in the same family as the Cobras. They live in trees in Africa.

By Roberta A. Kayne, Courtesy of Fort Worth Zoo

By Jeffrey M. Howland

▲ Coral Snakes are very shy snakes that usually hide during the day. It is rare for a person to be bitten by one unless the snake is handled in some way.

Which snakes live in trees?

A large number of snakes spend most of their lives in trees, such as the Long-Nosed Tree Snake.

By Jeffrey M. Howland

▲ Many tree snakes, like this Long-Nosed Tree Snake, drink drops of water off leaves, or even off their own bodies.

Which snakes live in water?

Many snakes can be found in or around water, but Sea Snakes and the unusual Tentacled Snakes very seldom come out of the water onto land.

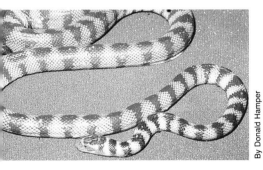

◄ Many Sea Snakes are awkward or even helpless on land but are able to move quickly and gracefully in the water.

▲ Tentacled Snakes are able to close off their nostrils to keep water out.

Which snakes burrow underground?

Many snakes, such as the Hognose Snake, are able to dig using their bodies in order to hide under the sand or soil. Some, such as the Shovel-Nosed Snake, have special scales on their head or body that help them burrow.

▲ Hognose Snakes have a rounded, blunt nose that helps them burrow underground in search of prey or to get out of the heat.

▲ When in loose sand, Shovel-Nosed Snakes move in a "swimming" motion. They can close off their nostrils to prevent sand from entering their bodies.

77

What are the most beautiful snakes?

That depends upon what colors you like. Snakes come in all colors—white, black, red, yellow, blue, green, orange, and everything in between.

Which snakes have strange-looking scales?

The Rough-Scaled Tree Viper looks as though it has shaggy or hairy scales. The Rhinoceros Viper has a horn on its nose. The Horned Desert Viper has horns over each of its eyes to keep the sand out when it's buried.

▶ **Rough-Scaled Tree Vipers are sometimes called "Hairy Vipers." They are great tree-climbers, and can even climb poles or stalks of tall plants that grow straight up.**

By Shay Hamper

▲ **Rainbow Boas get their name from their bright colors and scales that reflect sunlight like a prism. This causes their dazzling, shimmery appearance when in the sunlight.**

By David T. Roberts, Courtesy of Dallas Zoo

By Roberta A. Kayne, Courtesy of Fort Worth Zoo

▲ **Many of the Kingsnakes have colorful bands of black, white, red or yellow, which is why they are often confused with the venomous Coral Snake.**

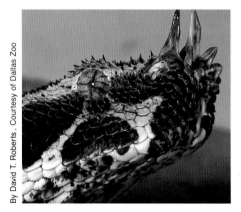

By David T. Roberts, Courtesy of Dallas Zoo

▲ **Rhinoceros Vipers have patterns with very distinct diamond, triangle, and other geometric shapes. They also have a large horn on their nose.**

What are the rarest snakes?

There are some snakes that have only been seen a few times. They are considered rare. The Chinese White-Headed Viper is one of the rarest snakes known. Snakes that are albino, such as the Albino Ringnecked Snake are not found very often, either.

By David T. Roberts, Courtesy of Dallas Zoo

By Thomas Wright

▲ The Indian Python is now protected by international laws. It became endangered because so many thousands were killed for their skins.

▲ Ringneck Snakes normally have colored undersides that they display when they defend

◄ Very little is known about the habits of the Chinese White-Headed Viper, because it has only rarely been seen. One of its unusual features is its white eyes.

Which snakes are endangered?

There are, unfortunately, several species that are now considered Endangered and could become extinct some day. The Indian Python and the San Francisco Garter Snake are just two of them.

themselves. Albino Ringneck Snakes hardly resemble the ordinary ones at all.

By James F. Brown, Courtesy of Fort Worth Zoo

▲ The San Francisco Garter Snake is now endangered due to changes in the parts of California in which it lives.

Acknowledgments

We would like to thank Sheila Anne Barry for encouraging us to write a children's book—we would never have thought it a feasible project without her enthusiasm.

Special recognition goes to our great photographers: David Roberts, Jim Brown, Roberta Kayne, Jeffrey Howland, Donald and Shay Hamper, and Tom Wright, as well as Bob Clark, Alan Zulich and Joe Pierce for their support. Thanks also to CPI Photo.

Our heartfelt love goes out to our families—Sherrie Stoops, Alesha Stoops, Liz Monger, Corrine Konz, Uncle Norman Kayne, Al and Lorraine Lajoie, and Heather and Melissa Benvenuti.

Thanks to all the professionals who assisted with questions: San Antonio Zoo, Tulsa Zoo, National Zoo, Seattle Zoo, Fort Worth Zoo, Dallas Zoo, and Kerry King.

And special thanks to the nurses and physicians at the Phoenix Children's Hospital Intensive Care Nursery.

Index

Albino snakes, 9, 13, 68, 79
Anal Plate, 21
Anti-venom, 70
Attraction, male-female, 48

Ball, rolling into, 61
Basking, 7
Birth, 50–55
Biting, 60, 65
Blindness, 31
Body, snake's, 14–27
Bones in back, 23
Burrowers, 26, 77

Cloaca, 43
Cold-blooded, 6, 7, 53
Coloration, baby to adult, 57; protective, 61
Colors, seeing, 31
Competition, for mate, 49

Death, 12
Digestion, 42–43
Drinking, 42; see Water

Ears, 32
Eating habits, 34–43
Egg layers, 50–55
Eggs, 51–55
Endangered species, 71, 79
Extinction, 70–71
Eyelids, 30
Eyes, 30–31

Family, definition of, 72
Fangs, 38, 40–41, 64–65, 68
Fat, getting, 37
Fear, 60, 69
Feeling, 33
Food, 34

Hatching, 55
Hearing, 32
Heat, ability to detect, 33
Hemipenes, 44–46, 49
Herpetologist, 13
Hissing, 61, 63
Horns, 78

Instinct, 56

Jacobsen's organ, 32
Jaw, 39

Killing of snakes, 70
Knots, tying self in, 26

Life span, snake's, 12
Lizard, difference between snakes and, 32
Lungs, 39

Mating, 46–50
Mice and rats, eating, 66, 68, 69
"Milking" the snake, 68
Muscles, 22, 23, 27
Musk spray, 62

Names, common and scientific, 73
North Pole, 7
Nose, used for digging, 26, 77; used in hissing, 63

Overeating, 37

People, relations with, 68, 71
Pits, heat-sensing, 33
Playing dead, 61
Poisonous snakes, 64–65, 69
Pregnancy, 50
Prey, 32, 33, 34–41; attracting, 75
Protected species, 71

Rarity, 70, 79
Rattling, 61, 62
Reproduction, 44–57
Reptiles, 6
Roads, snakes resting on, 12

Safety with snakes, 64
Saliva, different from venom, 41
Scales, 16–22, 31, 33, 62, 78
Self-defense, 58–65
Senses, 28–33
Serpentine wriggle, 24
Sex, how to tell which, 44
Shedding, 18, 31
Skin, absorbing water through, 42; shedding, 18, 31
Skull, 23
Sleeping, how to tell if, 30

Smell, sense of, 32; of musk, 62
Species, definition, 72
Spurs, 44, 45–46
Staring, 30
Strength, 27
Striking, 60
Swimming, 25

Tail, 21; males' longer, 47; prehensile, 27
Throwing up, 43
Tongue, 32
Taxonomists, 73
Teeth, 40
Temperature, body, 7, 8
Trees, climbing, 25, 76
Turtles, as prey, 75

Underground snakes that go, see Burrowers
Undersides, 61, 79
Urine, 43

Venom, 38, 40, 41
Veterinarian, 13

Wastes, 21, 43
Water, 76, 77; see Drinking

Yawning, 40, 42

Zoologist, 13